A STICK and a FIRE

The Best Way to Cook

Naturally, the secret to a good fire is using dry wood, preferably some that has been cut and drying for more than a year – it's easier to light and burns better and longer.

Get your fire started with some crumpled newspaper, dry wood shavings, or commercial fire starters. Add dried twigs and a few smaller branches. As things get going, add split wood to build up heat. For shorter cooking times *(when food just needs to be heated through)*, you can cook over some flames. The ideal heat for longer cooking times *(for dough and raw meat for instance)* occurs once you have achieved nice white, hot coals.

ISBN-13: 978-1-56383-627-5
Item #2919

Printed in the USA

www.cqbookstore.com

gifts@cqbookstore.com

Distributed By:

 Products

507 Industrial Street
Waverly, IA 50677

 CQ Products

 CQ Products

 @cqproducts

 @cqproducts

A stick and a fire – what more do you need?!

Pick a Stick

For authentic stick-cooked food:

- Choose long, sturdy, green twigs *(not dry ones)* so they won't break easily or catch on fire.
- Find those that are long enough to keep you away from the fire and sturdy enough to support the food.
- Whittle away the bark at the smallest end and sharpen to a point.

To use purchased sticks:

- Look for long roasting forks or sticks which come in a wide variety of shapes and sizes or regular metal skewers. Using short skewers will usually require a cooking surface such as a metal grate.
- Thick, heavy cooking sticks work well for heavy, sturdy foods; use thinner ones for light-weight, small, or delicate food.
- To keep food from spinning, use flat skewers, two side-by-side thin ones, or use a roasting fork with closely placed tines.

Stick Smarts

When assembling food on a stick, leave a little space between foods that require slow, even cooking *(like dough or raw meat)*.

If you don't want to hold food while you cook it, set a grate over the fire and lay the skewered food on top. A camping grate with legs or a grill grate work well. If you don't have a grate, use rocks to prop the food up over the fire!

Foil can be your best friend when campfire cooking. Use it to line your cooking grate for easy clean-up. Or wrap food in foil and pierce the foil with your cooking stick; hold over the fire to cook hobo-style.

Grab a stick and build a hot little fire!

Tropical Turkey Tzatziki

1 C. coconut milk
1 T. minced garlic
1 T. brown sugar
2 tsp. ground turmeric
1½ tsp. salt
1 tsp. ground cumin
½ tsp. ground ginger

½ tsp. ground coriander
¼ C. chopped fresh cilantro or chives
1½ to 2 lbs. turkey tenderloin
Lemon and lime slices
Tzatziki Sauce *(recipe below)*

Ahead of time, in a big resealable plastic bag, combine the coconut milk, garlic, brown sugar, turmeric, salt, cumin, ginger, coriander, and cilantro or chives; turn to mix. Cut the turkey into strips, ¼" to ½" thick and about 1" wide and add them to the bag. Seal the bag and chill for 2 hours.

Weave the turkey strips onto cooking sticks alternating lemon and lime slices between the loops and set on a greased grate over medium embers until cooked through, turning to brown both sides.

Serve with Tzatziki Sauce.

Tzatziki Sauce: Stir together 2 (5.3 oz.) containers *(about 1⅓ C.)* plain Greek yogurt, 1 small cucumber *(diced & patted dry)*, the juice of 1 lemon, 2 T. chopped fresh dill, 1 T. minced garlic, and salt and black pepper to taste.

Toasted Fruit & White Chocolate

Place 1 C. white chocolate chips in a small aluminum pan; cover with foil and set near the fire to melt. Stir in 1 tsp. vegetable oil and keep warm. Cut pears, bananas, apples, and pineapple into chunks; dip into orange juice and thread onto cooking sticks, alternating with fresh blackberries and regular marshmallows if you'd like. Sprinkle everything with a little cinnamon. Hold over medium-hot embers for a couple of minutes, turning frequently. Dip the fruit into the melted white chocolate for a decadent sweet treat!

Campin' Seafood Dinner

Ahead of time, in a big resealable plastic bag, combine 2 T. vegetable oil, 1 T. lemon juice, 1 T. soy sauce, ½ tsp. minced garlic, ¾ tsp. ground ginger, ¼ tsp. onion powder, and ⅛ tsp. black pepper; seal the bag and shake to combine. Add 1 lb. sea scallops *(cut in half if large)*; seal, toss to coat, and chill for several hours. Discard marinade and thread scallops onto cooking sticks along with fresh pineapple and zucchini chunks. Cook over medium-hot embers until scallops are done, basting frequently with soy sauce and/or lemon juice.

Rosemary Chicken Skewers

2 T. plain yogurt

1½ tsp. minced garlic

¾ tsp. salt

1 T. finely chopped fresh rosemary *(or 1 tsp. dried)*

1½ tsp. finely chopped fresh oregano *(or ½ tsp. dried)*

¾ tsp. lemon juice

Olive oil

1 lb. boneless, skinless chicken breasts, cubed

1 red onion, quartered

Cherry tomatoes

Kalamata olives

Ranch dressing for serving

Ahead of time, in a big resealable plastic bag, combine yogurt, garlic, salt, rosemary, oregano, lemon juice, and 2 teaspoons oil; seal the bag and shake to blend. Add the chicken and the onion and toss in as many tomatoes and olives as you'd like; seal the bag, turn to coat, and chill overnight.

Discard the yogurt mixture and shake off any excess from the food. Alternately thread chicken, onions, tomatoes, and olives onto cooking sticks and hold over hot embers until the chicken is done, turning to brown both sides.

Serve with dressing. De-licious!

TIRED OF HOLDING THAT COOKING STICK OVER THE FIRE? SIMPLY SET IT ON AN OILED RACK PLACED ABOVE THE FIRE. NO RACK? PROP THE STICK ON A ROCK AND HOLD THE HANDLE END WITH YOUR FOOT. YOUR CAMPFIRE. YOUR RULES.

Sweet Potato Wedges – 3 Ways

MAKES 18

Basic Potato Prep

Scrub 3 large sweet potatoes and parboil until crisp-tender; drain and set aside until cool enough to handle. Slice each potato into six thick wedges *(leaving the skin on)* and coat as directed for each recipe on the following page.

Slide coated sweet potatoes crosswise onto side-by-side cooking sticks and set on a greased grate over medium-hot embers. Cook until tender, turning as needed to brown both sides.

Serve with the dip or sauce indicated in each recipe.

Cinnamon Sweets

To coat prepped sweet potatoes, toss parboiled wedges in a mixture of 3 T. olive oil, ¼ tsp. pumpkin pie spice, ⅛ tsp. cinnamon, and ⅛ tsp. nutmeg.

Cinnamon Dip: Mix 4 oz. cream cheese *(softened)*, 1 tsp. each brown sugar and maple syrup, and ⅛ tsp. each pumpkin pie spice and cinnamon.

Sweet & Spicy Wedges

To coat prepped sweet potatoes, toss parboiled wedges in a mixture of ¼ C. olive oil, 2 T. brown sugar, 1 T. each smoked paprika and sea salt, 2 tsp. chili powder, and ½ tsp. cayenne pepper.

Creamy Maple Sauce: Mix ½ C. sour cream, ¼ C. mayo, 2 T. maple syrup, and salt and black pepper to taste.

Curried Sweet Dippers

To coat prepped sweet potatoes, toss parboiled wedges in a mixture of 1½ tsp. curry powder, ½ tsp. cayenne pepper, and salt and black pepper to taste.

Cilantro Yogurt Sauce: Mix 1 C. plain Greek yogurt, 3 T. chopped fresh cilantro, 1 T. chopped fresh mint, the zest and juice of 1 lime, 2 tsp. honey, and ¼ tsp. salt.

Strawberry Meringue Bites

Place 1 C. chocolate candy wafers in a small aluminum pan; cover with foil and set near the fire to melt. Once melted, dip whole fresh strawberries partway into the chocolate and set upside-down to harden a bit. Dip the berry into marshmallow fluff *(or swirl it on using a knife)* and push a cooking stick through the stem end. Hold over medium-hot embers, turning as needed until the fluff is nice and toasty. Mmmm...

Jamaican Jerk & Melon

Ahead of time, mix 2 T. vegetable oil and 4 tsp. Jamaican jerk seasoning in a big resealable plastic bag. Cut 1½ lbs. boneless, skinless chicken breasts into ½ x 1½" chunks and cut a yellow onion and 3 or 4 pablano peppers into 1½ to 2" chunks; add everything to the bag, seal, and turn to coat. Chill at least 30 minutes. Cut cantaloupe and honeydew melon into 1½ to 2" chunks and alternately skewer onto cooking sticks with the chicken (*pieces folded in half*), the onion, and the peppers. Hold over medium-hot embers until cooked through, turning to brown evenly. Toward the end of cooking, brush with a mixture of 1½ tsp. honey and 1½ tsp. vegetable oil. Drizzle on a little honey and sprinkle with more jerk seasoning before serving if you'd like.

Loaded Pizza Sticks

1 (13.8 oz.) tube refrigerated pizza crust dough

Flour, optional

Olive oil

Italian seasoning

Grated Parmesan or Romano cheese

1 (19 oz.) pkg. cooked Italian sausage links, cut into chunks

Small whole mushrooms

Cherry tomatoes

1 or 2 onions, cut into chunks

1 or 2 green bell peppers, cut into chunks

1 (3.5 oz.) pkg. pepperoni slices

Pizza sauce, warmed, optional

Press out the pizza dough on a floured or oiled surface to make a 9 x 12" rectangle; brush with olive oil and sprinkle with Italian seasoning and cheese. Cut crosswise into 12 strips, 1" wide.

Push one end of a dough strip onto a long cooking stick, then alternately thread on sausage, mushrooms, tomatoes, onions, bell peppers, and several pepperoni slices, threading the dough strip back onto the stick several times in between to secure. Wrap the end of the dough strip around and over the tip of the stick one last time, pinching well to seal. Repeat with the remaining ingredients.

Hold over medium embers, rotating slowly until golden brown all around and the dough is cooked through.

Serve with warmed pizza sauce if you'd like.

Whenever you're cooking dough over the fire, the trick is to cook slowly. Cook too fast and the dough won't be done in the middle, and that makes for unhappy campers. Patience just takes a little practice.

Italian Meatball Subs

1½ lbs. ground beef

1 C. panko bread crumbs

4 eggs

½ C. milk

¾ C. grated Parmesan or Romano cheese, plus more for sprinkling

1 tsp. onion salt

1 tsp. minced garlic

1 T. dried parsley

1 T. dried basil

1 onion, cut into chunks

4 to 6 sub buns

1 C. spaghetti sauce, warmed, optional

Ahead of time, mix ground beef, bread crumbs, eggs, milk, cheese, onion salt, garlic, parsley, and basil until well combined. Roll the mixture into 1½" balls and chill for several hours. Keep meatballs chilled until ready to cook.

Thread several chilled meatballs onto a cooking stick *(leaving a little space in between so they cook evenly)* and thread the onion chunks onto a separate stick. Cook over hot embers until meatballs are done and onions are crisp-tender and lightly charred, turning occasionally to brown all sides.

Serve meatballs and onions on buns with warm spaghetti sauce and a sprinkling of cheese.

USING A WOODEN STICK FOR COOKING THESE MEATBALLS WORKS WELL SINCE THE MEAT CLINGS TO IT.

Cajun Shrimp & Sausage

Ahead of time, whisk together ⅓ C. mayonnaise, 1 T. lemon juice, and 1 T. Cajun seasoning; chill until needed *(up to 2 days)*. Mix 2 tsp. olive oil and 1 T. Cajun seasoning in a big resealable plastic bag. Using paper towels, pat dry 1 lb. raw shrimp *(40 to 50 ct., peeled & deveined)* and add to the bag; seal the bag and turn to coat. Slice 1 (12 oz.) pkg. fully cooked Cajun-style sausage into rounds the same thickness as the shrimp. Alternately thread shrimp and sausage onto cooking sticks and hold over medium-hot embers until cooked and hot. Serve with the chilled dipping sauce. Hoo-Yah!

Berry-Mallow Puffs

Separate biscuits from a 7.5 oz. tube of refrigerated biscuits (10 ct.) and flatten each; sprinkle with cinnamon-sugar. Flatten a regular marshmallow and set it in the center of the biscuit. Add 1 or 2 fresh blackberries or raspberries *(cut in half if large)* or a few blueberries; sprinkle with a little orange zest. Fold the biscuit around the filling, pressing seams firmly to seal. Insert a cooking fork through the center of the biscuit. Cook slowly over warm embers until brown on the outside and no longer doughy in the center, rotating often to brown evenly. Eat carefully – it'll be hot – but oh, so enjoyable!

Savory Steak & Veggies

⅔ C. lemon juice

¼ C. vegetable oil

4 tsp. Worcestershire sauce

2 tsp. paprika

2 tsp. minced garlic

1 tsp. sugar

1 tsp. salt

¼ tsp. hot pepper sauce

1½ lbs. beef sirloin steak

2 onions

2 green bell peppers

½ to 1 lb. fresh whole mushrooms

Ahead of time, stir together the lemon juice, oil, Worcestershire sauce, paprika, garlic, sugar, salt, and pepper sauce; pour ½ cup of the mixture into a big resealable plastic bag and pour the remainder into a separate small container.

Cut the steak into 1" cubes and add them to the bag with the marinade; seal and turn bag to coat. Chill for at least 2 hours but no longer than overnight.

Cut onions and bell peppers into chunks. Discard the marinade from the bag and alternately thread beef, onion, bell peppers, and mushrooms onto a cooking stick.

Hold over hot embers until the steak reaches desired doneness, turning and basting frequently with the reserved marinade.

You wanna cook over a fire? Bring plenty of matches and keep them dry by storing them in plastic containers rather than in matchboxes. There's nothing worse than rubbing sticks together forever trying to get your fire going.

Veggies with Cilantro-Lime Butter

Olive oil

1 tsp. garlic powder

2 tsp. Italian seasoning

Salt and black pepper
  to taste

Tiny potatoes

Fresh veggies such as sweet
  corn, zucchini, yellow
  squash, red onion, bell
  pepper, mushrooms, and/or
  cherry tomatoes

Cilantro-Lime Butter
  (recipe below)

In a big resealable plastic bag, mix ¼ cup oil, garlic powder, Italian seasoning, salt, and pepper. Parboil potatoes until crisp-tender; drain, cool, and add to the bag. Cut fresh veggies into 1½" pieces as needed and add them to the bag with the potatoes; toss to coat.

Alternately thread the food onto cooking sticks and hold over a cooking fire, turning often until lightly charred.

Spread Cilantro-Lime Butter over the hot veggies. *(Form any leftover butter into a log, wrap in plastic wrap, and chill until needed again.)*

Cilantro-Lime Butter: In a small bowl, mix ½ C. softened butter, ¼ C. packed finely chopped cilantro, zest and juice from 1 lime, and 1 tsp. salt.

23

Piña Colada Tres Leches Dessert

In a resealable plastic bag, combine ½ C. sweetened condensed milk, ½ C. evaporated milk, ½ C. coconut milk, ½ tsp. cinnamon, and 2 beaten egg yolks. Seal the bag and shake to blend. Cut about ¾ lb. unsliced French bread into 1" cubes and add them to the bag; seal and turn to coat. Push the coated bread cubes onto cooking sticks alternately with pineapple chunks and hold over warm embers until the bread is no longer "eggy" in the middle. Transfer bread and pineapple to bowls and top with toasted coconut and cherries *(and if you have whipped cream, add that too)*.

Great Little Greek Sandwiches

Spread 1 sourdough bread slice with hummus; cut into quarters. Top two of the quarters with 1 cucumber slice, deli-sliced roast turkey, a big roasted red pepper piece, and sliced provolone cheese; add the other bread quarters, hummus side in, to create two sandwiches. Butter the outside of the bread and push the sandwiches onto cooking forks, making sure everything gets skewered in place. Hold over hot embers until the bread is toasted and the cheese begins to melt. Open wide!

Buttons & Ribbons

⅓ C. white wine vinegar

⅓ C. olive oil

1 tsp. dried lemon peel

½ tsp. salt

½ tsp. black pepper

½ tsp. celery seed

1 medium zucchini

1 small eggplant

½ lb. whole mushrooms

4 to 6 hot dogs, cut into chunks

Ahead of time, in a big resealable plastic bag, mix the vinegar, oil, dried lemon peel, salt, pepper, and celery seed. Cut zucchini and eggplant into long ribbons, about ¼" thick; cut eggplant ribbons in half lengthwise if necessary so they're about the same width as the zucchini ribbons. Add the ribbons to the bag along with the mushrooms and hot dogs; seal the bag and turn to coat. Chill for at least 2 hours.

Discard the marinade and weave strips of vegetables onto cooking sticks, alternating the mushrooms and hot dog pieces between the loops. Cook over medium embers until vegetables are crisp-tender, turning often.

S'mores Galore

Try these delicious ideas, and you may just find a new favorite s'more.

Faux Mint Oreo: chocolate graham crackers, thin mint candies, toasted marshmallow

Cinnfully Hazelnut: cinnamon graham crackers, Nutella, toasted marshmallow

Cheesecake: graham crackers, ready-to-eat cheesecake filling, cherry or blueberry pie filling, toasted marshmallow

Cookielicious: a toasted marshmallow sandwiched between two of your favorite cookies

White Chocolate-Berry: graham crackers, white chocolate candy pieces, toasted marshmallow, fresh berries

Peeps: at some point, you've gotta build a s'more with Peeps

Funky Monkey

Load up a chocolate graham cracker with Nutella, banana slices, and a toasted strawberry marshmallow. Add another cracker and you've got yummy goodness!

Camper's Dream

Start with a regular graham cracker and smear it with raspberry jam; add dark chocolate pieces and top it off with a toasted marshmallow. Press down with another cracker and be prepared for ooey-gooey deliciousness!

Sundae S'more

What do you get when you sandwich some cookies & cream candy bar pieces, a toasted marshmallow, and chopped maraschino cherries between two oatmeal cookies? Bliss! Pure bliss!

Pork 'n' S'more

A basic s'more goes one step further. Toast a marshmallow and layer it between two regular graham crackers along with milk chocolate candy bar squares and crisply cooked bacon. Hog heaven!

Popcorn Pouches

Pour about 1 T. vegetable oil and 2 T. popcorn kernels on an 18″ square of heavy-duty foil. Bring the corners of foil together to make a pouch and seal the edges closed, leaving room for popcorn to pop and expand. Tie both ends of the pouch to a cooking stick with string. Hold the pouch over a cooking fire and shake until corn is popped. Cool slightly before opening. Make your popcorn extra-special by adding any of the following:

   a) Melted butter and salt
   b) M&Ms and roasted peanuts or cashews
   c) ½ tsp. taco seasoning and a handful of shredded cheddar cheese
   d) ½ tsp. garlic salt, onion salt, sugar, or your favorite seasoning
   e) 1 square melted white almond bark

Campfire Cinnamon Spirals

Remove and separate rolls from a 12.4 oz. tube of refrigerated cinnamon rolls (8 ct.) and set aside enclosed frosting. Unroll each cinnamon roll and twist the dough around a cooking stick. Pinch together at the end so it clings to the stick during cooking. Heat slowly over warm embers, turning occasionally until the outside is golden brown and the inside is no longer doughy. Slide the rolls off the sticks and frost.

DOUGH CLINGS WELL TO A WOODEN COOKING STICK, MAKING IT EASIER TO COOK.

Sesame-Ginger Brat K'Bobs

¾ C. purchased sesame-ginger marinade

¼ C. lime juice

2 bell peppers, any color

1 red onion

1 zucchini and/or yellow squash

1 (14 oz.) pkg. fully cooked brats

Small whole white mushrooms

Ahead of time, pour the marinade and lime juice into a big resealable plastic bag. Cut the bell peppers, onion, squash, and brats into chunks and add them to the bag along with the mushrooms; seal the bag, turn to coat, and chill for 30 minutes.

Alternately thread the marinated food onto cooking sticks. Hold over a cooking fire until heated through, turning and brushing with the marinade occasionally.

THE JOY OF COOKING KABOBS IS THE OPPORTUNITY FOR NEARLY ENDLESS CUSTOMIZATION. CHOOSE FOODS WITH SIMILAR COOKING TIMES OR SIMPLY THREAD EACH TYPE OF FOOD ONTO ITS OWN STICK AND COOK SEPARATELY; THAT WAY, IF ONE ITEM GETS DONE QUICKER THAN THE REST, YOU'RE NOT STUCK WITH OVERCOOKED FOOD. PERFECT!

Chinese Pork Ribbons

3 T. soy sauce

2 T. rice wine vinegar

2 T. olive oil

1 tsp. honey

2 to 3 tsp. Chinese
  5-spice blend

½ to 1 tsp. red pepper flakes

1 tsp. garlic salt

1 lb. pork tenderloin

Bottled peanut sauce

Ahead of time, in a big resealable plastic bag, mix the soy sauce, vinegar, oil, honey, 5-spice blend, pepper flakes, and garlic salt. Remove excess fat from the tenderloin and cut the meat into 12 strips, ¼" thick and about 5" long. Add the strips to the bag; seal, and turn to coat. Chill for at least 4 hours but no more than 24 hours.

Discard the marinade and thread pork strips accordion-style onto cooking sticks. Set sticks on an oiled grate over medium-hot embers and cook until the meat is done.

Serve with peanut sauce.

DIY Chinese 5-Spice Blend: To make just enough for this recipe, mix 1 tsp. cinnamon, 1 tsp. crushed anise seed, ¼ tsp. crushed fennel seed, ¼ tsp. black pepper, and ⅛ tsp. ground cloves.

Fish 'n' Foil

Ahead of time, in a big resealable plastic bag, mix ⅓ C. olive oil, ¼ C. lemon juice, 1 tsp. dried basil, ½ tsp. dried thyme, ¼ tsp. salt, ¼ tsp. black pepper, and 1 tsp. garlic powder; add 1 lb. thawed cod fillets. Seal the bag, turn to coat, and set aside for 30 minutes. Line four 12 x 24" pieces of heavy-duty foil with parchment paper; spritz with cooking spray. Peel 1 spaghetti squash, remove seeds, and cut into ¼"-thick crosswise slices; lay a few slices on each lined foil piece. Add fresh green beans to each, drizzle with olive oil, sprinkle with salt and garlic powder, and top with some fish. Close parchment/foil around the food, sealing with tight, heavy folds; push the ends of a cooking fork through each pack, right below the folds. Hold over hot embers until cooked and tender.

Simple Eggs 'n' Bells

Cut 2 bell peppers *(any color)* in half crosswise and scrape out all the seeds and membranes, leaving four shells. Push the ends of a long cooking fork carefully through each half so they hang like baskets. Crack an egg or two into each basket; hold over warm embers until egg is cooked. Season with salt, black pepper, and dill weed to taste. For an omelet, whisk an egg with your favorite ingredients *(try shredded cheese, ham, and veggies)*, then pour it into the pepper and cook as directed.

TO PREVENT SCORCHING THE PEPPER DURING COOKING, COVER THE OUTSIDE OF THE PEPPER HALF IN FOIL. THEN PUSH THE FORK THROUGH BOTH THE FOIL AND THE PEPPER; ADD THE EGG AND COOK AS DIRECTED.

Balsamic Steak Bundles

2 tsp. butter

2 T. finely chopped shallot

¼ C. balsamic vinegar

2 T. brown sugar

¼ C. beef broth

2 carrots

1 zucchini

1 red bell pepper

½ lb. asparagus, trimmed

1½ lbs. sirloin steak

Worcestershire sauce

Salt and black pepper to taste

Mesquite steak seasoning

Ahead of time, melt the butter in a small pan and add the shallot; cook until softened. Stir in the vinegar, brown sugar, and broth. Bring to a boil, boiling until liquid is reduced to about half. Meanwhile, cut the carrots, zucchini, and bell pepper into matchsticks; toss into boiling water along with the asparagus and parboil for a few minutes, then drain.

Cut the steak into eight equal pieces and pound ⅛" to ¼" thick; drizzle with a little Worcestershire sauce and let stand for 10 minutes. Top each steak piece with some of the parboiled vegetables and season with salt and pepper.

One at a time, roll the steak around the vegetables and thread onto side-by-side cooking sticks, catching the ends of the steak to secure; repeat until all the bundles are skewered. Set aside 2 tablespoons of the balsamic mixture and brush the remainder over the bundles. Sprinkle with steak seasoning.

Cook the sticks on an oiled grate over hot embers, until steak is cooked to your liking, turning to brown both sides.

Brush with set-aside balsamic mixture before serving.

Precooked rice that you can purchase in a bag at the grocery store is a great staple to take along on camping trips. Simply heat it up over the fire *(or use a microwave if you have one).*

Mushroom Delight

¼ C. olive oil

¼ C. lemon juice

A small handful of fresh parsley, finely chopped, or 1 T. dried parsley

1 tsp. sugar

1 tsp. salt

¼ tsp. black pepper

¼ tsp. cayenne pepper

1 tsp. minced garlic

1 T. balsamic vinegar

1 lb. whole white or baby Portobello mushrooms

Ahead of time, in a resealable plastic bag, mix the oil, lemon juice, parsley, sugar, salt, black pepper, cayenne pepper, garlic, and vinegar. Cut the mushrooms in half lengthwise through the stem and add to the bag; seal, turn to coat, and chill for 45 minutes.

Carefully slide the mushrooms onto thin cooking sticks and set on a greased grate over a cooking fire for several minutes on each side until hot, softened, and slightly browned. Just like the name says – delightful!

Sunrise Sausages

Separate rolls from a 12.4 oz. tube of refrigerated cinnamon rolls (8 ct.) and unroll them, making ropes; set aside the frosting. Push both tines of a cooking fork through a precooked smoked sausage; wrap a cinnamon roll rope around it, pushing tightly to secure. Repeat with seven more sausages and the remaining ropes. Cook slowly over warm embers until the rolls are no longer doughy, turning to brown all sides; frost.

Sausage Dunkers: In a tall, narrow drinking glass, mix 1 C. biscuit baking mix, 1 T. sugar, ⅓ C. milk, and 1 egg until well blended. Cut a 14 oz. precooked smoked sausage ring into chunks and push a cooking stick through the length of each; dip into batter to coat. Cook above hot embers until golden brown. Serve with maple syrup.

Cheesy Bacon Dogs

Slice 1 string cheese stick lengthwise into four pieces. Cut a slit in each of 4 hot dogs, from one end to the other, without cutting through the bottom. Place one cheese piece into the slit of each hot dog and roll the whole thing in brown sugar. Wrap a bacon strip around each one to hold in the cheese; secure with toothpicks. Push both tines of a cooking fork through each hot dog bundle. Cook very slowly over hot embers until bacon is cooked, turning to brown all sides. Remove toothpicks and sing cheesy bacon dog praises.

Frank Kabobs: Cut hot dogs and whole dill pickles into equal sized chunks; thread alternately onto a cooking stick and heat over the fire until browned to your liking. Slide the food onto a bun. Yum-yum.

Pork & Apple Sticks

1 lb. pork tenderloin

Salt to taste

1 green bell pepper

1 onion

2 Gala apples

Lemon juice

2 tsp. melted butter

½ C. applesauce

¼ C. finely chopped walnuts

2 T. brown sugar

Remove excess fat from the tenderloin and cut the meat into 1" cubes; season with salt. Cut the bell pepper, onion, and apples into chunks; dip apples in lemon juice. Alternately thread the meat, vegetables, and fruit onto cooking sticks.

Stir together the butter, applesauce, walnuts, and brown sugar and brush liberally over the food.

Set on an oiled grate and cook over hot embers until the pork is done, turning to brown both sides.

Buffalo Biscuit Cups

1 (16.3 oz.) tube refrigerated biscuits (8 ct.)

2 lbs. boneless, skinless chicken thighs, cooked & shredded

½ C. finely chopped carrots

½ C. finely chopped celery

½ C. finely chopped red onion

4 to 5 T. buffalo sauce

1 tsp. lemon juice

Salt, black pepper, and garlic powder to taste

Chopped tomatoes

Shredded cheddar cheese

Blue cheese dressing

These biscuit cups can be filled with just about anything. Try tuna salad, scrambled eggs, taco filling—even green bean casserole! Be creative and enjoy!

On the end of a long, thick stick or wooden dowel, create a "cup" 3" to 4" in diameter by wrapping with layers of foil; cover with a longer piece of foil, wrapping and twisting it down and around the dowel to hold it in place. Spritz the cup lightly with cooking spray. *(Having more than one of these is ideal!)*

Separate biscuits; one at a time, lay them on a flat surface and press into a thin circle *(without tearing them)*. Lay the biscuit over the end of the foil cup and press gently. Keep remaining biscuits chilled until needed.

Hold the biscuit above warm embers until nicely browned on the outside and no longer doughy in the middle, rotating often. Repeat with remaining biscuits. *(If you're having trouble getting the cups done in the middle, remove from the dowel once browned and set on a rack, open side down, above hot embers; it'll only take a few minutes.)*

Meanwhile, stir together the chicken, carrots, celery, onion, buffalo sauce, lemon juice, salt, pepper, and garlic powder. Spritz a big piece of foil with cooking spray and dump half the chicken mixture in the center; bring the edges of the foil up around the filling and crimp several times to seal, making a thick, heavy fold. Repeat with more foil and the remaining chicken mixture. Push a cooking stick through the foil below the fold of each pack; hold over the heat until the filling is warm.

Divide the mixture among the biscuit cups and top with tomatoes, cheese, and dressing.

State Fair Smoked Chops

Ahead of time, in a big resealable plastic bag, mix ¼ C. each brown sugar and honey, 1 T. vegetable oil, the juice of 1 lime, and 1 tsp. red pepper flakes. Remove the bone from 2 large 1"-thick fully cooked smoked pork chops and cut the meat in half. Add the meat to the bag, seal, and marinate for at least 20 minutes. Discard the marinade and push each pork chop half onto a sturdy cooking stick. Hold over medium embers until sizzling and heated through, rotating to brown all sides. Eat right off the stick like at the fair or be a little more civilized and use a fork and knife.

Prosciutto & Mozzarella

Carefully push cherry tomatoes and mini marinated mozzarella balls onto flat cooking sticks, weaving strips of prosciutto in between; brush with Italian dressing. Hold over medium embers until the tomatoes have softened slightly, the prosciutto is starting to brown around the edges, and the mozzarella is just beginning to melt. A quick and easy appetizer to snack on any time.

Camping Eclairs

1 (3.4 oz.) pkg. instant pudding mix *(we used French vanilla, but use what you like)*

1¾ C. milk

1 tsp. vanilla or almond extract, optional

1 (7.5 oz.) tube refrigerated biscuits (8 ct.)

Spray whipped cream

Thick hot fudge sauce or chocolate frosting

Ahead of time, whisk together pudding mix, milk, and extract until smooth. Transfer to a resealable plastic bag; seal and chill until needed.

Cover about 8" at the end of a 1" diameter cooking stick or dowel with foil; grease it well. For each eclair, press two biscuits together and flatten well. Wrap the dough around the foil end of the stick to make a tube about 4" long; pinch edges together tightly to seal.

Hold the stick over warm embers and cook slowly until brown on the outside and no longer doughy in the middle. Carefully slide the biscuit tube off the stick.

Cut off a corner of the bag containing the pudding and pipe pudding into each tube; fill with whipped cream. Top with fudge sauce or frosting and dig in.

You can't rush it when cooking dough over the fire, but the time it takes pays off big-time when you take a bite of these eclairs!

Fireside Salmon Tacos

1 T. paprika

1 tsp. cayenne pepper

1 tsp. dried thyme

1 tsp. ground cumin

½ tsp. onion powder

½ tsp. garlic powder

1 tsp. salt

¼ tsp. black pepper

1 lb. thick skin-on salmon fillets, cut into chunks

Vegetable oil

Cherry tomatoes

1 red onion, cut into chunks

Small flour or soft corn tortillas

Shredded lettuce or cabbage

Guacamole

Lime wedges

Mix paprika, cayenne, thyme, cumin, onion powder, garlic powder, salt, and pepper. Push salmon into the mixture to coat all sides well. Rub oil over tomatoes and onion chunks. Alternately thread salmon, tomatoes, and onions onto flat cooking sticks and cook over hot embers until salmon is done, carefully turning once partway through cooking.

Meanwhile, char some tortillas over the fire if you'd like.

Remove the food from the skewers. Discard the skin from the salmon and flake the meat. Fill the tortillas with the cooked food, lettuce, and guacamole.

Squeeze lime juice over the tacos, fold, and eat. Campfire food never tasted so good!

Candy-Mallow Poppers

For each popper, first push a regular marshmallow onto a cooking stick. Then add your favorite mini chocolate candy bar right behind the marshmallow, keeping them as close to the pointed end of the stick as possible. Toast carefully over warm embers *(you don't want that delicious candy bar melting into the flames)*. When the marshmallow is golden brown, slowly slip it over the candy and pull both of them off together. The candy bar sets nicely inside the marshmallow and softens slightly, creating a yummy pop-in-your-mouth treat. Pop carefully – they're piping hot!

Grilled Cheese Sandwiches

For each sandwich, cut off and discard the crust from a good-sized slice of sandwich bread *(ours was whole grain, which worked well)*; roll or press flat. Put a few cheese curds *(we used chipotle flavored)* down the center of the bread and roll up tight, sealing the cheese inside. Push the ends of a cooking fork through the sandwich, catching the sealed edges; secure with toothpicks if needed. Brush melted butter over the outside and heat slowly over hot embers until the bread is toasted and the cheese is soft and melty. Remove from the stick and eat immediately. If you're a ketchup-on-grilled-cheese kind of person, go ahead and dip your sandwich in some of the red stuff. We won't judge.

Bacon-Bacon-Bacon

Stuffed Dills

Cut 5 or 6 regular whole dill pickles in half lengthwise and scoop out a little from the centers, leaving a boat shape; pat dry with paper towels. Mix 4 oz. cream cheese *(softened)*, ¾ C. finely shredded cheddar cheese, and 1 tsp. minced garlic until well combined. Divide the mixture among half the pickles and cover with the other half; cut bacon strips in half and wrap one piece snugly around each pickle to hold the halves together. Slide onto long cooking sticks, catching the ends of the bacon to secure. Cook over hot embers, turning often, until bacon is done and everything is hot.

Bacon & Asparagus

Discard the hard ends from medium-size fresh asparagus spears and cut spears in half crosswise. Cut bacon strips in thirds and wrap one piece around two asparagus pieces; thread onto two side-by-side flat cooking sticks, catching the ends of the bacon to secure. Repeat with as many asparagus bundles as you need *(you can fit several on each stick)*. Spritz with cooking spray and sprinkle lightly with grated Parmesan cheese and black pepper. Cook over medium embers, turning several times, until bacon is done.

Wrapped Cantaloupe

Use a melon baller to scoop the fruit from a cantaloupe. Wrap one parcooked bacon strip *(or a partial strip, depending on size)* around each cantaloupe ball and push onto flat cooking sticks *(or two side-by-side ones)*, catching the ends of the bacon to secure. Heat over hot embers, turning often, until bacon is crisp.

Cheesy Baby Reds

16 tiny red potatoes

¼ C. olive oil

Garlic salt

Black pepper

½ lb. farmer's or Havarti cheese, cut into small squares

Chopped fresh or dried chives, optional

Sour cream, optional

Ahead of time, parboil the potatoes until just barely crisp-tender; set aside until cool enough to handle.

In a big resealable plastic bag, mix the oil, 1 teaspoon garlic salt, and 1 teaspoon pepper. Slice off a little from one side of each potato to create a flat top and add the potatoes to the bag; seal, toss to coat, and chill for 1 hour.

Thread the coated potatoes onto flat, sturdy cooking sticks with all the flat sides facing the same direction; set on a grate, flat sides down over very hot embers. Cook until nicely browned. Flip so flat tops face up and set a cheese square on each. Let the cheese melt, then sprinkle with chives and a little more garlic salt and pepper.

Serve with sour cream if you'd like.

Teriyaki Meatball Spears

Cut 1 fresh pineapple, 1 white onion, and 1 each red and green bell pepper into bite-size chunks. Alternately thread the food onto cooking sticks with fully cooked frozen meatballs *(from an 18 oz. pkg., thawed)*. Hold over a cooking fire, rotating every few minutes until everything is hot and lightly charred, brushing with warmed apple or apricot jelly the last few minutes.

Baked Apples

Place sugar in a small aluminum pan and stir in a little cinnamon and ground nutmeg *(and just a pinch of cayenne pepper if you'd like a surprising little kick)*; set aside. For each apple, push a sturdy cooking stick into the bottom of your favorite kind of baking apple, about halfway through. Hold above hot embers, rotating occasionally, until the skin browns and loosens. Pull the apple away from the heat, use a sharp knife to carefully remove the skin, and then roll the apple in the sugar mixture until evenly coated. Eat it right off the stick or slice and serve with whipped cream, ice cream, or marshmallow fluff – whatever you have available. Any way you slice it *(or don't)*, it's wonderful!

All-In-One Breakfast

Tiny potatoes

Oranges

Green bell peppers

Kumquats

Brown-and-serve
 sausage links

Pineapple chunks

Orange marmalade, warmed

Ahead of time, parboil potatoes for just a few minutes, until slightly tender.

Cut oranges into wedges *(don't peel)*, cut bell peppers into 1" pieces, and cut sausage links into chunks. On a stick, alternately skewer potatoes, oranges, bell peppers, whole kumquats, sausage, and pineapple. Brush marmalade liberally over the food.

Hold over hot embers until sausages are hot, fruit is lightly charred, and vegetables are crisp-tender, turning and brushing occasionally with marmalade. For good measure, brush a little more marmalade over everything just before serving.

Kumquats are probably the only citrus-type fruit you don't peel to eat – just pop 'em into your mouth! Their sweet-tart flavor mellows a bit when cooked over a fire.

Index